Saving Our Seabirds

HELPING AT-RISK & ENDANGERED SPECIES

Saving Our Seabirds

A collection of fine-art drawings
for coloring, stories of each seabird,
and messages on climate change

Drawings by
Lynn Matsuoka

Tiger & Dragon
Publishing

It's bigger than a coloring book, grander than the concept of relaxation and focus. This is a call to action, to awareness, a plea for awareness in action, a plea to connect to our earth, to our world, to our future.

LM

Dedicated to my beloved Muriel and Sandy.
I know you would love this.

TABLE OF CONTENTS

ACKNOWLEDGEMENTS

This may appear to be a very simple book, but it took the support of many people over the last year to accomplish it. After two major losses in my life following decades of great accomplishments, suddenly I felt lost.

Fortunately I somehow found Steve Harrison, through whose organization, Quantum Leap, I found myself surrounded by professional and supportive coaches for writing, organizing my path forward, and many other things I needed to do.

Judy Cohen, one of my coaches, first informed me there was such a thing as "adult coloring books", a platform to use for the endangered bird drawings I had been doing. I immediately set out to create this book. Thank you so much for the direction to create this project.

I cannot express enough thanks to Martha Bullin, who advised me on style, content, helping me think, last minute organization and wonderful writing edits.

Thanks to Raia King for promotional direction and support, and to many others in QL, all of whom are the best one can find.

Many thanks to Project Puffin Executive Director Dr.Stephen Kress, scientist, writer and advocate for all seabirds, for direction and critique, and for writing the stories of the endangered birds for the book. And to Director Tiffany Huenefeldt for her informed support.

I so appreciate the enthusiasm and support of Frank Quevido, Executive Director of the South Fork Natural History Museum on Long Island, for this book and it's message.

Thanks to my very patient book designer Christy Collins who walked me through this new experience and put up with so many delays.

To the brilliant digital designer/ IT expert Lonson MacCarger, if my drawings look good at all, it is thanks to your incredible patience and great skill.

To those who contributed their important and expert thoughts on Climate Change, thank you so much for taking the time from very busy lives to support this book's message.

Dr. Phil Agrios, the personal and business consultant, knows just how to cut through one's agitation and fluster, and many times brought me back to earth. You are a treasure.

Great appreciation to the Andrew Sabin Family Foundation for supporting Wildlife Conservation and their support of this book.

In Japan, where I'm known for my drawings & paintings of SUMO and KABUKI Theater, the media called me *"the Degas of Sumo and Kabuki "*. Still interested in theater & sports, I add Birds to this list. They are not only so beautiful and more intuitive than us humans, they are a precious resource in this world and are at our mercy. We must protect them, and then we will be protecting ourselves, if that is what people need to know to become pro-active.

I THANK EVERYONE who does whatever they can to provide shelter, clean water and safety to all birds. And *please* consider their migratory routes before constructing hazards in their paths.

And thanks to my 2 sons who constantly goose me to "get that book done!"

Lynn Matsuoka, Sag Harbor, N.Y. 2019

ARTIST'S NOTE

Seabirds live mostly out at sea, far away. The mission of this book is to bring them closer to us and to create a tactile, even emotional connection to them through the meditative focus of coloring these carefully created drawings. I hope this book will inspire more people to do the things necessary to help them (and us) by making the necessary changes to our lifestyles to slow and stop the onslaught of climate change.

I first heard about the tragedy of puffins dying out off the coast of northern Norway some years ago due to climate change. At that time, the seas had warmed 1 1/2 degrees. The baby Puffins, called "pufflings", can feed only on slim little fish that in turn feed on plankton. The warming seas were now either killing the plankton so the slim fish the puffins needed for their pufflings had disappeared, or forcing the plankton to lower depths, the slim fish with them, making it more difficult, even impossible for the puffins to find them As a result, the little pufflings were starving and dying. The adult puffins eventually stopped laying eggs because they knew their pufflings would not survive. This is just one tragedy killing the birds, among so many around the world.

Icebergs melting into the sea at alarming rates, threatening the extinction of thousands of species, and coastal cities around the world facing rising sea levels. Stories like these are in the news every day. We must all become aware and proactive, and do our part to protect our earth and the precious species living here.

I have kept the drawings in this first edition simple, without extraneous detail. I want the drawings and your work on them to be as beautiful as possible, while still maintaining each bird's distinctive markings.

Please feel free to add details and colors to make these drawings your own. The sky might be a simple light or dark blue, as a backdrop for your chosen seabird. Or, you may want to color an orange sky, to contrast with the bird's colors and make it more exciting. Be free, fly with the bird over the sea and imagine the ocean air. See what he or she sees.

As color was not possible in this edition, please see my website for a picture of each bird, so you can see the actual colors. Soon there will be a video on the website on several coloring techniques for you to try. www. hamptonsartist.com

Several special people have written messages for this book to share their knowledge and suggestions about actions we can take to protect seabirds and our planet. We can do better tomorrow than we did yesterday in caring for our environment.

Thank you for buying this book and helping to save our endangered seabirds, their habitats and our Earth!

Lynn Matsuoka,
New York JUNE 2019

Introduction
CELEBRATING SEABIRDS

Stephen Kress, Ph.D. co-author of *Project Puffin: The Improbable Quest to Bring a Beloved Seabird Back to Egg Rock*

Water covers about two thirds of Earth, providing a living habitat for creatures ranging in size from tiny plankton to enormous whales. Yet all of these live under water, largely mysterious to people. In contrast, seabirds greet us at the coasts and at sea. They live above the waves, yet they are dependent on what they find under the water. Some can fly for weeks far from land and others can plunge hundreds of feet under the water. Their beauty and family life are compelling, yet mostly unknown to most people because they spend their lives in places where people seldom venture and when they do come to nest, they usually choose the most remote islands or cliff sides. This coloring book by famed artist Lynn Matsuoka celebrates the lives of seabirds through art and surprising facts about their lives and the threats that they now face. This is important because about a third of the World's 300 plus seabird species are threatened with extinction because of things that humans are doing to our water world.

As top predators in the ocean food web, seabirds are valuable indicators of marine health and climate change. Seabirds also improve our lives by offering a source of beauty and inspiration for the millions of people who live, work or visit coastal and marine habitats. However, these are difficult times for seabirds. Though some have survived since the days of dinosaurs, now many are threatened with extinction. Globally, seabird abundance has dropped by 70% in the last 60 years. This decline is a major warning that life at sea has become much more difficult not only for seabirds, but for all that depend on the oceans- including people.

Fortunately, seabirds have proven highly responsive to conservation activities conducted around the globe, such as protection and restoration of breeding islands, reduction of incidental catch in fishing gear, and conservation of forage fish. If we take care of seabirds, we can address most of the conservation problems of our time.

Climate Change

Burning fossil fuels like coal and petroleum releases 'greenhouse gases' such as carbon dioxide. This warms air and oceans, leading to less plankton, the principle food for the small 'forage fish' that feed seabirds. Warming water also causes more rainfall in some areas and droughts in other areas, hurricanes and other extreme weather. Warmer weather is also causing polar ice to melt and flood coastal areas as ocean levels rise. Seabirds feel the impact of these changes at sea and their nesting homes.

Sustainable Fisheries

Collapses in forage fish, squid, and other prey populations directly affect seabirds. Too often forage fish are overfished due to lack of management, ignoring the needs of seabirds, marine mammals, and predatory fish. Policies that protect fish and programs to recommend sustainable fish for human consumptions are helping to make a difference.

Marine Protected Areas

Marine Protected Areas (MPAs) are key to sustaining quality habitats for seabirds, fish, and other marine life. There is strong interest in Latin America (e.g., in Chile) to identifying and creating new MPAs in alignment with the Convention of Biological Diversity, which calls for 10% of the ocean to be protected by 2020.

Plastics and Oil

Almost all plastic eventually finds its way to our oceans, floating and blowing from coastal communities. Once in the ocean, it breaks up into tiny 'microplastics' that stay in the ocean forever, breaking into smaller bits that are now found from surface to deep water and worldwide as they are transported by global ocean currents. Seabirds perish from plastics by choking, entanglement and by finding less to eat as the plastics affect every level of the ocean food web. Reducing and replacing plastics is the best approach to managing this growing problem. Seabirds are also especially vulnerable to oil pollution, as even a small patch on their feathers breaks their waterproofing, creating exposure to frigid waters. Reducing use of petroleum products reduces risk to seabirds.

Project Puffin and the Audubon Seabird Restoration Program

Since 1973, Project Puffin has worked to restore colonies of Atlantic Puffins and other seabirds to historic nesting islands on the Maine Coast where extensive hunting led to the loss of most puffins and other seabirds by 1900. Through long-term management, Project Puffin has brought puffins back to several Maine islands, currently protecting about 1,300 pairs. The Seabird Restoration Program shares methods learned in Maine with other countries to help them create new colonies of rare and endangered seabird species. Today, Audubon's seven Maine field stations protect most of the state's rare and endangered seabirds while helping other countries to protect their seabirds.

To follow the success of Project Puffin and to sign up for our newsletter, please visit www.projectpuffin.org. Here you can learn how to:

- Make a donation in honor or memorial for someone special,
- Adopt a puffin for yourself or others
- Take a Maine puffin watch tour,
- Watch live puffin cams
- Shop in our on-line store for puffin gifts
- Take part in five-day resident natural history programs for adults, teens and families at Hog Island Audubon Camp.

Take Action for Seabirds

Small actions by individuals really do help. Together, we can make a big difference.

- Discuss why you care about climate change with others.
- Use less fossil fuels with efficient vehicles and appliances.
- Turn down air conditioning and heat.

- Turn off lights in rooms when not in use.
- Use public transit.
- Reduce lawns and lawn mowing.

Reduce use of plastic as most of it eventually gets into the oceans

- Never release helium filled party balloons (especially metallic coated balloons) as most eventually end up at sea where they can choke seabirds, marine mammals and turtles.
- Avoid using plastic straws, plastic utensils and one-use plastic bags. Explain to servers why you care.
- Pick up and recycle plastics along roadsides, walkways and public areas.

Eat sustainable seafood

- At restaurants and markets, reference the Monterey Bay Aquarium's *Seafood Watch* program: https://www.seafoodwatch.org/ Download the app.
- At restaurants, ask your server where seafood comes from. Starting conversations about sustainable seafood helps makes restaurants aware that people care.
- Look for the MSC (Marine Stewardship Council) when purchasing seafood.

Create Bird Friendly habitats

- Avoid fertilizers and yard pesticides that poisons backyard wildlife and run off that eventually reaches oceans.

Vote for elected officials that understand the urgency of ocean conservation.

Become a Seabird Advocate!

THE MESSAGE IS CLEAR

By Frank Quevedo, Executive Director
South Fork Natural History Museum (SOFO)

Throughout our history, we look to birds as bioindicators of the health of our precious planet. They tell us when seasons are changing, notify us when habitats are diminishing, help us understand our own species, and delight us with beautiful songs every day. But today, they have an urgent message for us, and need our help now, more than ever.

The urgent message is very clear...birds are on the go, as many of them are changing their migration patterns due to climate change impacts. Nearly half of the bird species in the United States and Canada are seriously threatened by rising temperatures. If nothing is done to decrease this threat, many of the bird species we've come to know will be gone forever.

Each bird species is uniquely adapted to its surroundings...including temperature, precipitation and the changing seasons. They have become finely tuned to a set of environmental conditions, so that everything, such as physiology, behavior and genetics allows a bird to be successful in its environment. But when rising greenhouse gases change the climate, the conditions that birds depend on are thrown into disarray. Adapting to these rapid changes can be catastrophic for many bird species and their survival might be in question.

Birds may be forced to look for habitat in unfamiliar places, away from their normal ecosystems. As they search for a new habitat, they will face new competition for limited food supply, resources and encounter new predators or fierce competitors which will make it difficult for their survival. It's a serious message we've been given. So, what can we do to help?

There's something all of us can do in our individual lives and in our communities to make it a better place for birds and for people. First, we need to take action and reduce carbon pollution which causes global warming and we need to get involved to protect and preserve the habitats birds need today and in the future.

This wonderful book, "Saving Our Seabirds" by Lynn Matsuoka, is a great way to begin the process of restoring and protecting our planet for future generations.

THE COLORING PAGES

A Collection of Original Seabird Drawings with
descriptions of the birds by Dr. Stephen Kress

ATLANTIC PUFFIN
Fratercula arctica
Status: Vulnerable

Habitat: Atlantic Puffins are ocean-going seabirds found only in the North Atlantic. They spend their first several years at sea far from sight of land. They are wonderfully adapted for their ocean going life with adaptations such as completely waterproofed feathers, ability to drink salt water and a built in sense of direction that would make an explorer envious.

Amazing facts:
- Puffins spend their first two or three years floating at sea without stepping foot on dry land.
- They can hold as many as sixty tiny fish in their beaks at once.
- Puffin beaks glow under ultraviolet light.
- They may retain the same nesting burrow and mate for ten or more years.
- When chasing prey under water, they use partly open wings, reminiscent of a penguin's flippers.

Threats: Puffin populations are declining through much of their range, especially where warming oceans force forage fish to deeper depths or further from nesting islands. When this happens, puffins struggle to find enough food and adults and chicks may perish. Their survival depends on:
- Slowing global warming so that oceans remain productive places for puffins and people.
- Better fishery management that leaves more fish in the sea for puffins and other wildlife.
- Cleaner seas with less plastic and oil pollution.

Management:
- Secure fishing regulations that protect forage fish and sustainable fish populations.
- Restore more puffin colonies at secure places, especially islands with high terrain to offer protection from sea level rise that can flood nesting pairs and their young.

Atlantic Puffin

ATLANTIC PUFFIN

Fratercula arctica
Status: Vulnerable

Habitat: Atlantic Puffins are ocean-going seabirds found only in the North Atlantic. They spend their first several years at sea far from sight of land. They are wonderfully adapted for their ocean going life with adaptations such as completely waterproofed feathers, ability to drink salt water and a built in sense of direction that would make an explorer envious.

Amazing facts:

- Puffins spend their first two or three years floating at sea without stepping foot on dry land.
- They can hold as many as sixty tiny fish in their beaks at once.
- Puffin beaks glow under ultraviolet light.
- They may retain the same nesting burrow and mate for ten or more years.
- When chasing prey under water, they use partly open wings, reminiscent of a penguin's flippers.

Threats: Puffin populations are declining through much of their range, especially where warming oceans force forage fish to deeper depths or further from nesting islands. When this happens, puffins struggle to find enough food and adults and chicks may perish. Their survival depends on:

- Slowing global warming so that oceans remain productive places for puffins and people.
- Better fishery management that leaves more fish in the sea for puffins and other wildlife.
- Cleaner seas with less plastic and oil pollution.

Management:

- Secure fishing regulations that protect forage fish and sustainable fish populations.
- Restore more puffin colonies at secure places, especially islands with high terrain to offer protection from sea level rise that can flood nesting pairs and their young.

Atlantic Puffin

AUSTRALASIAN GANNET
Morus serrator

Status: Not threatened

Habitat: Gannets are members of the Pelican order, related to boobies. The three gannet species nest in cold waters of the northern and southern hemisphere. The Australasian Gannet is most common in New Zealand, nesting in dense colonies on the mainland. The largest colonies have 5,000 pairs. They also nest in southeast Australia and Tasmania.

Amazing Facts:
- Gannets rear just one chick per year.
- If they lose their egg, they can lay a replacement egg in a month.
- They keep the chick warm on top of their webbed feet.
- Flocks of gannets plunge vertically like so many torpedoes to capture fish.
- Some birds retain the same mate for live, return to the same nest site, but divorces are known.

Threats: Gannets require large amounts of fish near their nesting colonies. Excessive fishing and warming oceans from climate change can make it difficult to raise young. When food is scarce, both parents must leave the nest to search for food, leaving the chick alone at the nest and vulnerable to other gannets seeking nesting places. Warming seas are forcing gannets to feed further from their colonies. Wind farms near gannet colonies are another cause of concern.

Management:
- In New Zealand, gannet decoys and audio recordings are helping to start new colonies in safe places, which spreads risk.
- Responsible placement of wind turbines reduces risk to flying gannets.

Australasian Gannet

BLACK FOOTED ALBATROSS
Phoebastria nigripes

Status: Near Threatened

Habitat: More than 95% of Black-footed Albatross nest in the remote Northwestern Hawaiian Islands, with the largest colonies on Midway Atoll and Laysan Island. They spend most of their life at sea, capable of drinking saltwater and finding food with their excellent sense of smell.

Amazing Facts:
- An elaborate dance with sounds and movements, likened to bows, head bobbing and mutual preening synchronizes the nesting season.
- For nearly three weeks after hatching, one parent stays with the new chick, while the other usually feeds far from the nesting island.
- It takes four to five months of regurgitated feedings for the chick to fledge.
- The fledging is on its own after it leaves the nesting island.

Threats:
- Ocean level rise from climate change threatens to destroy most Black-footed Albatross colonies.
- Plastics that are picked up with food and fed to chicks This may save some chicks from choking and dyeing.
- Many species of albatross are vulnerable to take a brush up course. Albatross of many species frequently become entangled in fishing gear and drown.

Management:
- Devices on fishing boats are helping to reduce entanglement by adult and fledgling albatross.
- Decoys and audio recordings are encouraging albatross to nest on high ground.
- Fenced enclosures offer protection from dogs and other mammal predators at some colonies.

Black Footed Albatross

BLACK FOOTED ALBATROSS
Phoebastria nigripes

Status: Near Threatened

Habitat: More than 95% of Black-footed Albatross nest in the remote Northwestern Hawaiian Islands, with the largest colonies on Midway Atoll and Laysan Island. They spend most of their life at sea, capable of drinking saltwater and finding food with their excellent sense of smell.

Amazing Facts:

- An elaborate dance with sounds and movements, likened to bows, head bobbing and mutual preening synchronizes the nesting season.
- For nearly three weeks after hatching, one parent stays with the new chick, while the other usually feeds far from the nesting island.
- It takes four to five months of regurgitated feedings for the chick to fledge.
- The fledging is on its own after it leaves the nesting island.

Threats:

- Ocean level rise from climate change threatens to destroy most Black-footed Albatross colonies.
- Plastics that are picked up with food and fed to chicks This may save some chicks from choking and dyeing.
- Many species of albatross are vulnerable to take a brush up course. Albatross of many species frequently become entangled in fishing gear and drown.

Management:

- Devices on fishing boats are helping to reduce entanglement by adult and fledgling albatross.
- Decoys and audio recordings are encouraging albatross to nest on high ground.
- Fenced enclosures offer protection from dogs and other mammal predators at some colonies.

Black Footed Albatross

BLUE-FOOTED BOOBY
Sula nebouxii

Status: Least Concern

Habitat: These plunge-feeding seabirds of tropical waters are related to the gannets of colder oceans. Blue-footed Boobies are famed for their powder-blue feet and their high-stepping display. These signature dances attract and hold the attention of their mate.

Amazing Facts:
- As many as 200 boobies can feed together by plunging into schools of anchovies and sardines.
- Boobies can plunge from 60 feet above the surface and hit the water at speeds of 60 miles per hour.
- Once a pair forms, they may stay together for life.
- Females are larger than males and typically dive in deeper water.

Threats:
- The Galapagos Islands of Ecuador were home to about half of the world population with 20,000 birds. However, the colonies there have declined greatly in recent years due to a drop in numbers of sardines.
- Insufficient sardines do not kill adults, but parents have a hard time finding enough food for chicks and without replacements, the population is declining
- Ingestion of plastics is another threat to boobies.

Management:
- Tracking studies with GPS tags are demonstrating where boobies are going to find food in an effort to create marine protected areas that are safe for forage fish and seabirds.
- Preventing plastics from polluting the oceans is key to protecting boobies and other seabirds.

Blue-Footed Booby

BLUE-FOOTED BOOBY
Sula nebouxii

Status: Least Concern

Habitat: These plunge-feeding seabirds of tropical waters are related to the gannets of colder oceans. Blue-footed Boobies are famed for their powder-blue feet and their high-stepping display. These signature dances attract and hold the attention of their mate.

Amazing Facts:
- As many as 200 boobies can feed together by plunging into schools of anchovies and sardines.
- Boobies can plunge from 60 feet above the surface and hit the water at speeds of 60 miles per hour.
- Once a pair forms, they may stay together for life.
- Females are larger than males and typically dive in deeper water.

Threats:
- The Galapagos Islands of Ecuador were home to about half of the world population with 20,000 birds. However, the colonies there have declined greatly in recent years due to a drop in numbers of sardines.
- Insufficient sardines do not kill adults, but parents have a hard time finding enough food for chicks and without replacements, the population is declining
- Ingestion of plastics is another threat to boobies.

Management:
- Tracking studies with GPS tags are demonstrating where boobies are going to find food in an effort to create marine protected areas that are safe for forage fish and seabirds.
- Preventing plastics from polluting the oceans is key to protecting boobies and other seabirds.

Blue-Footed Booby

COMMON MURRE
Uria aalge

Status: Least Concern

Habitat: The Common Murre is one of the most numerous seabirds in the Northern Hemisphere, numbering about 21 million birds. It lives in large colonies in the Canadian Maritimes and is especially abundant in Alaska and south to central California. Common Murres spend most of their year at sea and come ashore only to lay their single egg.

Amazing Facts:
- Murres lay large, colorful eggs and they can recognize the distinct pattern of their egg and distinguish it from neighboring eggs.
- They can dive to over 300 feet in pursuit of herring, anchovies and other small forage fish, usually bringing their chick a single fish from each dive.
- When murre chicks are just 3 to 4 months old, the flightless chicks leap from cliffs or scramble to the shore to follow their father to sea where he feeds them for the next 1 to 2 months.

Threats:
- Murres are vulnerable to warming waters, which can reduce the abundance of suitable fish.
- Predators such as gulls and eagles can sometimes spook large numbers of murres from their nests, leading to a cascade of eggs falling from cliff side nesting ledges.
- Murres are especially vulnerable to oil spills; even a small patch of oil can break their water-proofing and cause them to die from exposure.

Management:
- Boaters should keep a safe distance from nesting islands to reduce disturbances, especially during incubation and chick rearing days during spring and summer.
- Protection of nesting islands and feeding locations from oil and chemical spills.
- Sustainable fisheries for herring, anchovies and other forage fish.

Common Murre

ELEGANT TERN
Thalasseus elegans

Status: Near Threatened

Habitat: There are only five colonies of Elegant Tern and a world population of only 90,000. They nest only in southern California and northwestern Mexico. After the summer nesting season, they winter south along the coast of South America to Chile, preferring shallow estuaries and bays.

Amazing Facts:
- Unlike some smaller terns that are very aggressive near their nests, Elegant Terns rely on their sheer numbers for defense. They sometimes nest near more aggressive Heerman's Gulls to protect chicks from predators such as Western Gulls.
- Chicks stay in the nest for about a week after hatching, then move to groups called a creche where adults take turns guarding the group of chicks.
- 90% of all Elegant Terns nest on Isla Rasa in the Sea of Cortez.

Threats: Food near nesting islands is key to the survival of this species, but fish is becoming scarce due to fisheries and warmer waters, sea level rise and other impacts of climate change.

Management:
- Protection of nesting islands from human disturbance and introduced predators is helping to protect Isla Rasa.
- Enhanced protection of anchovies and other forage fish is necessary to insure there is ample food, especially for chicks.
- Removal of invasive mammals such as cats and rats is also important to insure that chicks are safe.
- Plans are taking shape to use decoys and audio recordings to create a new colony in southern California on an artificial island.

Elegant Tern

ELEGANT TERN
Thalasseus elegans

Status: Near Threatened

Habitat: There are only five colonies of Elegant Tern and a world population of only 90,000. They nest only in southern California and northwestern Mexico. After the summer nesting season, they winter south along the coast of South America to Chile, preferring shallow estuaries and bays.

Amazing Facts:

- Unlike some smaller terns that are very aggressive near their nests, Elegant Terns rely on their sheer numbers for defense. They sometimes nest near more aggressive Heerman's Gulls to protect chicks from predators such as Western Gulls.
- Chicks stay in the nest for about a week after hatching, then move to groups called a creche where adults take turns guarding the group of chicks.
- 90% of all Elegant Terns nest on Isla Rasa in the Sea of Cortez.

Threats: Food near nesting islands is key to the survival of this species, but fish is becoming scarce due to fisheries and warmer waters, sea level rise and other impacts of climate change.

Management:

- Protection of nesting islands from human disturbance and introduced predators is helping to protect Isla Rasa.
- Enhanced protection of anchovies and other forage fish is necessary to insure there is ample food, especially for chicks.
- Removal of invasive mammals such as cats and rats is also important to insure that chicks are safe.
- Plans are taking shape to use decoys and audio recordings to create a new colony in southern California on an artificial island.

Elegant Tern

HEERMAN'S GULL
Larus heermanni

Status: Near Threatened

Habitat: This is the only gull that breeds south of the United States and comes north during the nonbreeding season. Almost all Heermann's Gulls breed on Isla Raza in the Gulf of California. Here they nest in a huge colony that has a nesting population of about 150,000 birds. Also known as white-headed Gulls, they prefer coastal marine habitats.

Amazing Facts:
- This bird's population fluctuates wildly.
- Nests on hot desert sand.
- They can be aggressive, often chasing larger birds such as Brown Pelicans to take their food.
- Frequents wharfs and docks looking for food when not nesting.
- Its closest relative is the Lava (Dusky) Gull of the Galapagos Islands.

Threats: Their habit of nesting in one location makes them very vulnerable to predators, disease and local fisheries exploitation.

Management:
- Protecting Isla Raza from accidental introduction of rats, cats and other predators.
- Protecting the nearby fisheries to assure that the birds have ample food.
- Creation of additional colonies using decoys and sound recordings to reduce risk from predators or other surprising factors. .

Heerman's Gull

HEERMAN'S GULL
Larus heermanni

Status: Near Threatened

Habitat: This is the only gull that breeds south of the United States and comes north during the nonbreeding season. Almost all Heermann's Gulls breed on Isla Raza in the Gulf of California. Here they nest in a huge colony that has a nesting population of about 150,000 birds. Also known as white-headed Gulls, they prefer coastal marine habitats.

Amazing Facts:
- This bird's population fluctuates wildly.
- Nests on hot desert sand.
- They can be aggressive, often chasing larger birds such as Brown Pelicans to take their food.
- Frequents wharfs and docks looking for food when not nesting.
- Its closest relative is the Lava (Dusky) Gull of the Galapagos Islands.

Threats: Their habit of nesting in one location makes them very vulnerable to predators, disease and local fisheries exploitation.

Management:
- Protecting Isla Raza from accidental introduction of rats, cats and other predators.
- Protecting the nearby fisheries to assure that the birds have ample food.
- Creation of additional colonies using decoys and sound recordings to reduce risk from predators or other surprising factors. .

Heerman's Gull

PELAGIC CORMORANT
Phalacrocorax pelagicus

Status: Near Threated.

Habitat: These long-necked, graceful cormorants live along open, wind-swept coasts of Baja California and the southern tip of the United States where they often nest with other cormorants. They prefer the most steep and remote cliffs where they are safer from predators. Pelagic Cormorants typically hunt alone in heavy surf for crabs, marine worms and small fish.

Amazing Facts:

- They can dive in either shallow, marine water near beaches or they can plunge to 180 feet deep or more in search of small forage fish.
- They often feed in Kelp forests
- A close-up view shows that the Pelagic Cormorant is a magnificent rainbow of iridescent greens and blues.

Threats:

- Eagles and Western Gulls can harass nesting cormorants and force them off their eggs.
- Oil spills are a deadly threat to cormorants.

Management:

- Boaters should stay clear of cormorant nesting ledges as they can flush abruptly and knock their eggs and chicks into the sea.

Pelagic Cormorant

RAZORBILL
Alca torda

Status: Near Threatened

Habitat: Razorbills are the closest living relative to the now extinct Great Auk. They nest on remote North Atlantic islands in rock crevices. Unlike the flightless Great Auk, Razorbills are adept at flight and superb divers that are aided by using their half-extended wings- much as a penguin. About one million breeding pairs occur, with about 60-70% nesting in Iceland.

Amazing Facts:
- They use the same nesting burrow year after year.
- Razorbills are monogamous, choosing one mate for life.
- The pair may mate up to 80 times in a 30-day period and females may mate with other males.
- When fledging time comes, the father Razorbill leads the chick to sea before it can fly when it is just 17-23 days old.
- Lifespan is about 13 years, but one UK Razorbill lived to a record old age of 41 years.
- Razorbills feed within 7-8 miles of nesting islands; like their puffin cousins, they can bring home many small fish at once.

Threats: Given that Razorbills are concentrated in Iceland where warming seas are affecting forage fish, the future for Razorbills is at risk because the birds may lose their critical food supplies.

Management: Protection of forage fish populations by regulation of catch limits would help to ensure that enough fish are left in the sea for Razorbills and other seabirds.

Razorbill

ROSEATE TERN
Sterna douglassi

Status: Endangered in northeastern U.S. and Canada;
threatened in southeast U.S.

Habitat: Roseate Terns frequent marine intertidal habitats worldwide, especially in the tropical, equatorial regions. In the northeastern U.S., they usually nest with more abundant Common Terns.

Amazing Facts:
- Roseate refers to the bird having a pink breast during courtship.
- The beak turns from jet black with an orange base, to mostly orange with a black tip as the nesting season progresses.
- The body weight of an adult tern is about 3.2 oz.

Threats:
- Predators such as mink will kill nesting adults, chicks and eggs.
- Ocean level rise can flood nesting habitat
- Avian predators such as Herring and Great Black-backed Gulls, Great Horned Owls and Black-crowned Night-heron can decimate small colonies.
- Unsupervised people can flush them from their nesting islands, exposing embryos and small chicks to other islands where they might nest.

Management:
- Nest boxes in appropriate habitat.
- Management to prevent invasive plants from taking over habitat.
- Create new nesting colonies

Roseate Tern

GUEST MESSAGES

THE MOST IMPORTANT ISSUE OF OUR TIME

Susan Rockefeller, Chairwoman of Oceana's Ocean Council, award-winning documentary filmmaker, and so much more. Oceana.org

Climate change is the most important issue of our time. It has already created mass extinction of species as well as increased displacement of millions of people—a problem that will only grow worse with time. The solutions are within our grasp, but will require collaborative action between governments, businesses, NGOs, and individual citizens.

We have an opportunity to invest in a beyond-carbon economy and innovate for a future that will be better for human, animal, and planetary health. From energy to agriculture, transportation, health, education and housing, we can draw down our carbon emissions and work toward a circular, no-waste economy.

Climate change is a common threat and therefore an opportunity for all of us. We can make any of our daily choices—professional or personal—count for a cleaner, greener and more carbon-free planet. We all must work to create the future we want. This will take innovation, resilience and a willingness to imagine a future where climate change is acknowledged as our number one threat to existence and to design a future that reflects this reality.

MY CHALLENGE TO YOU

Dr.Paul Clapis , physicist, speaker, and lifelong resident of Connecticut.

I love walking barefoot along the beaches of my native Connecticut in the summer, feeling the cool, wet sand beneath my feet. I walk along the shoreline, watching the waves break and wash up and back, trying to guess if the tide is coming in or going out. As a scientist, I know that the tides are caused by the pull of invisible fingers of gravity from the moon and the sun, but that more significant motion is all but hidden in the movement of the surf, and soon my footprints will be washed away by the inexorable tide.

Every day we are reminded that the climate change tide is coming in, as inevitable and inexorable as the lunar tides. I can recall with a shudder the devastating effects of Hurricane Sandy, the tens of billions of dollars in damages, the thousands of homes damaged, and hundreds of thousands of residents who went without power for weeks. I think about the rapid changes in our seacoasts caused by rising global temperatures, and I've studied the research that shows the reasons why our warming Earth makes extreme weather more likely and more frequent.

Climate scientists have studied the history of climate change recorded in the ice fields of Greenland, they have monitored the temperature changes of the Earth, and studied the celestial motions of the sun and planets that influence the amount of sunlight bathing our world. They have spent tens of thousands of hours carefully constructing tests and examining the evidence to reach our current understanding of the impact of climate change. Scientists often devote a lifetime in pursuit of knowledge but you don't need a Ph.D. to understand the consequences, and you don't have to be a scientist to want your children and grandchildren to live a happy, healthy life.

My challenge to you

is to learn just one thing about climate change. Do your own reading about the key issues, then share with your friends what you know. That's how you can make a difference.

You can hone your critical thinking skills and ask questions whenever you read or hear something that you don't understand. Asking meaningful questions is the best way to learn (and it's an essential step toward thinking like a scientist).

Talk to your children, who probably know more about climate change than us. It's their future, after all, and they take it seriously. We can act as responsible custodians of our planet and vote for leaders who will help create change.

Every major political candidate has proposed (or will soon offer) their specific plans for dealing with climate change and its consequences. Some of the ideas are ambitious, but that may be precisely what's needed given the urgency of the timetable.

If we don't take action now, our beaches will be swept away by the rising sea levels, and our coastal communities will be damaged irreparably. The charm and character of our Northeastern heritage will be lost forever, and our grandchildren will never visit the sands where we once walked.

Paul Clapis is a physicist, speaker, and lifelong resident of Connecticut. He can be reached at pauljclapis@gmail.com.

DROWNING IN POTENTIAL OR THRIVING FOR OUR CHILDREN

Dr.Rod Wallace, consultant, economist, and speaker

A recent technology conference empowered me. Electric implants allow paralyzed people to walk and blind people to see. Virtual reality machines immerse students in three dimensional images of their own body. We can do *anything*.

A sign captures Eric Schmidt, the former CEO of Google, exclaiming, "We're entering the age of abundance!" because Eric knows that with today's technology, we can solve any problem. We can create any society we want!

When I get home, I skip up the stairs, running my fingers along the cool, wrought-iron railing. I pause in front of my son's room to watch the brown-haired, blue-eyed moppet sleep. Love and joy overwhelm me. I *can* create an environment that will support him.

But as I turn to leave, fear overcomes me. "What if I Fail? What if *WE fail?*" I'm terrified.

We are drowning in social problems. Culturally we suffer increasing loneliness, depression, and suicide. The American government features increasing gridlock and, since 1980, the first large, non-war debt ever. Over 60% of the US economy is dedicated to industries failing to consistently deliver our most basic needs, including:

○ Food that doesn't nourish us as it should: the obesity epidemic is now global, and levels of micronutrients are decreasing in our produce.
○ Healthcare on which Americans spend vast amounts, yet we have the shortest lives in the developed world. And they're getting shorter, as depression, suicide, opioids, and other poor lifestyle choices become growing problems.

- Education that pulls in ever-greater spending, yet huge portions of American college graduates cannot understand a simple table or make a cohesive argument.

And our environment could be on the edge of a devastating precipice.

But we don't have to drown. Our *children* don't have to drown. Technology delivers so much potential. And **_people_** can solve almost any problem, especially when we work together.

So, how do we begin the collaborative process that will solve our problems? By focusing on *each other*. In your personal life, engage the *people* around you. Put the phone away. Don't put your phone on the table, put it completely out of sight in your bag or pocket.

As a citizen, stay engaged and vote. Whether or not anyone is using high-tech approaches to influence a campaign, it's still the votes that matter, and you control your own.

In business, search for **meaningful profit**. As digital technology draws us increasingly into rapidly changing detail, take a step back to see the big picture. Find innovative approaches that help solve the social failures that surround you, and you'll likely find an approach that *also* benefits you and your investors.

Eliminating our social problems completely requires new insights, tools, and strategies that shift our complex systems. Yet choosing a *human, socially responsible, approach* is a critical first step everyone can take.

Our society cannot just survive. For the sake of our children, it must thrive.

Dr. Rod Wallace is a consultant, economist, and speaker who helps businesses make more money by solving society's big, systemic problems. A Fulbright Fellow, Rod earned his PhD at the University of Michigan and was an invited researcher at the Japanese Ministry of Economy, Trade, and Industry. He's also led billion dollar business initiatives worldwide, explored the impact of Artificial Intelligence on society, and is the author of the groundbreaking best-seller, *Drowning in Potential: How American Society Can Survive Digital Technology*. Reach Rod at Info@RodWallacePhD.com.

CLIMATE CHANGE INDUCED
DECLINE OF PUFFINS

Dr. Alfred K. Hanson, Chemical Oceanographer

In the spring of 2018 I visited Sag Harbor, NY and had the opportunity to meet Lynn Matsuoka, the artist and author of this very interesting and important book about seabirds. Lynn informed me that climate change induced changes in the coastal ocean were believed be responsible for the starvation and decline of the Puffin populations in the coastal waters off Norway. The scientific consensus seems to be that global warming of the coastal surface waters, is causing the displacement of the small fish populations, that the Puffins feed on, to distant locations. Meeting Lynn Matsuoka triggered my interest and I have been conducting some research on the phenomena. During August of 2018, I visited the Island of Runde and the Herøy - Fjord in Norway, that are important seasonal nesting areas for Puffins and other seabirds.

As a Chemical Oceanographer I conducted climate change related research for several years while I was at the University of Rhode Island, Graduate School of Oceanography, located on Narragansett Bay in Rhode Island, USA. In the late 1990's I was involved with research on nutrient gradients, thin plankton-rich layers and associated small fish populations, in a Fjord on OCRAS Island, in Puget Sound, Washington state. I believe that the ORCAS Island Fjord is very similar oceanographically (geology, physics, chemistry and biology) to the rocky Fjords in Norway, where the Puffins like to lay their eggs and raise their young. My evolving theory is that the phenomena of thin plankton-rich layers, is critically important for the biological food-web that the Puffins depend upon in Norway Fjords. If global warming of surfaces waters interferes with the formation, persistence and location of these food-rich thin plankton layers, and their associated small fish populations, then the Puffin population may starve.

Puffins can swim **underwater** and fly in the air. They have evolved their high-speed wings and their rudder like webbed feet to enable them to swim efficiently **underwater**, where they catch small fish including herring and sand eel. Reportedly, they can **dive** to a **depth** of 200 ft and can stay **underwater** for 20 to 30 seconds. Thin Plankton Layers are always embedded underwater within the thermocline. The warming of coastal surface waters causes the depth of the thermocline to be deeper in the water column. This could be a challenge to the Puffins, perhaps their preferred food fish, located near the Thin Plankton Layers, are there, but too deep to reach, catch and return with, during their 20-30 sec allotted dive time.

This is a very interesting and important environmental topic and I want to thank the talented artist Lynn Matsuoka, for introducing me to the plight of the puffins and other seabirds, which is rapidly becoming a critical global environmental problem.

Contact Information for Dr. Alfred K. Hanson;
Marine Research Scientist, Emeritus, University of Rhode Island, Graduate School of Oceanography,
Email: akhanson@uri.edu

Founder, Director: Center for Environmental Awareness, RI

President: SubChem Sensor Systems, Inc., Narragansett, RI (www.subchem.com) Email: hanson@subchem.com

THE SEAGULL'S TRAGIC LAMENT: TRASH KILLS

Dell Cullum, wildlife rescue responder and rehabilitator

We've all seen seagulls pulling trash from a lidless or mismanaged trash receptacle. It's often perceived that these winged beach scavengers will eat just about anything, and in most cases this notion is absolutely correct; however, that's not where this story ends.

I'm a wildlife rescue responder and rehabilitator in the oceanside town of East Hampton, on Long Island, in NY. I rescue, rehab, and in many cases bury dozens of seagulls each year that die from severe food poisoning, brought on by eating trash. Seagulls are not the easiest bird to rehab to begin with, but food poisoning to gulls more often results in a slow and painful death.

Let's think about a wild animal's behavior when introduced to non-native food. A great example is feeding bread to ducks or swans at a park or community duck pond. Tossing a single piece of bread into a pond full of hungry waterfowl will instantly create a frenzied charge of all ducks toward that piece. Throwing a peanut into a group of grey squirrels would cause the same turbulent results, and in most cases during this frenzy, one or more critters will get injured, scratched or bitten in an effort of being the one to reach that food first. Seagulls will do the same, although their feeding frenzies can be quite vocal as well.

What makes the gull unique is that they are scavengers of the highest level. They will eat anything, anytime, anywhere. In fact, those seagulls that feed from landfills and heavy food-waste trash areas simply stop eating their natural diet, like insects and fish, all together and survive off of trash. The majority of this food waste trash (french fries, ice cream, stale bread, etc., etc.,) isn't good for the humans it's meant for, so imagine what it does to the health of a bird. Unfortunately, their uncontrollable inability to avoid certain toxic edibles either leaves them poisoned or even worse, with a gullet full of undigestible debris that slowly starves or suffocates the bird. Scientists studying the contents in perished seagull stomachs have recently found drywall and small metal pieces among the contents which is suspected to come from landfills that share their waste stream with construction debris, two categories of waste that are often separated in recycling facilities.

Believe it or not, East Hampton Village actually puts their trash receptacles ON THE BEACH. Several cans remain in the normal location where the parking area meets the sand, but during the heavier populated (heavier trash flow) months they add dozens more half way closer to the water. These cans cannot be properly maintained throughout the season and often become overfilled, used for late night household dumping stations, abused by being knocked over or the lids being used for fire pits. It's actually quite a harmful decision and confusing for a Village who claims to be leading the way to a greener future. No matter how you look at it, allowing seagulls to consume our trash could potentially lead to lethal results. Could that be any worse? In fact it can.

Once the raccoons knock over the trash receptacles, and along with the seagulls feast on the remnants of waste, what they don't consume will certainly become slave to the elements. Shoreline breezes to full blown nor' easters transport this trash up and down our shoreline, but most often it ends up in the ocean. Ironically as our oceans are trying to cough up the debris we carelessly dumped into them a century ago, we continue to be careless on shore. Now for the coup de grace.

What happens in the life span of a gull between when it begins eating our trash, to the point in which the trash ultimately kills the gull? Let's just say, what goes around comes around. Scientists are now looking at the impact seagulls have on our water quality due to their excessive contribution of poop. Science has already found traces of toxic chemicals in seagull poop from our plastic-filled seas, but they have now found a huge link in those seagulls who primarily feed from trash or at landfills, redepositing toxic chemicals, nitrogen and phosphorus back into the water via their droppings. In 2018, a rough calculation concluded by Duke University's Wetland Center came up with a number of 1.4 million seagulls in the United States that live at landfills. As you can imagine, that's a lot of nitrogen and phosphorus that seagulls are collectively dumping. In water, it changes the chemical composition and could lead to more algae blooms, which kill other organisms in water body ecosystems.

Rather than struggling to keep our waters clean AFTER they've already been polluted, perhaps we can attack and eliminate the problem at the source, focusing on the trash.

In conclusion, it would seem best for both our health and the health of our wildlife and water quality to decrease the availability of trash waste for wildlife consumption.

The easiest change would be to eliminate all trash receptacles from being placed on the physical beaches. Even better, begin educating the community about the "Carry In - Carry Out" policy and practice. As far as trash availability at landfills, I suggest that recycling and refuse centers keep their transportable waste stream (trash that gets reloaded and transported to larger inland landfills) inside covered structures (as most already do); however, it would be further suggested that the doors be used more often in between dumps and loading. Leaving the doors ajar at these waste holding and loading facilities allows wildlife, particularly seagulls, access to the filth. Simply keeping the facility doors closed would end that problem.

MOST IMPORTANTLY, dispose of all trash and debris properly and in secured trash receptacles.

Participate in or start your own community or beach clean up. And lastly, spread the word. Trash & Litter is ugly, and it doesn't belong on our roadsides, parks or beaches.

Dell Cullum, Wildlife Rescue of East Hampton, NY
ImaginationNature.com, 631-377-6555 Kachina35@gmail.com

A MESSAGE FROM POET
LAURA DI FRANCO

Published poet and author, inspirational speaker, holistic physical therapist

Connect to the miracle
of your moment
with a deeper breath.

Let the morning songs
dance with your ears.

Watch the birds
float and soar;
turbo-feathered jets,
aerodynamic spirits,
resting in green-leaved canopies
between daily tasks.

They practice their mating calls,
make their beds,
feed their kids...
just like us

Trusting their wings to take them
where they need to go,
knowing their purpose
is to fly.

Birds have been special to me since I was a child. After my grandmother died Mom would say, "Oh, there's Grandma!" when she saw a bird perch on our wooden deck rail outside the kitchen window. Living in California offered us the opportunity to watch so many different birds do their thing. In the redwood trees, by the sea, along the bay…wherever we were there was always a new bird to gaze up at.

Later in life birds became a sign to follow my path and purpose. Teachers showed me books and I read about things like abundance and joy. I found the love of birds in the pages of poetry books and knew I wasn't alone in my wonder and awe.

Conservation of all living creatures, proof of the miracle of life, is something we should all embrace. Not only because our very lives depend on these creatures surviving, but because of what would become of our spirits in their absence. The birds, bees and other creatures we share this planet with help us believe in something bigger than ourselves. And with that belief there's hope.

Laura Di Franco, MPT is the owner of Brave Healer Productions and a powerhouse who writes to Feng Shui her soul. She's a 6-time published poet and author, inspirational speaker, holistic physical therapist and third-degree black belt in Tae Kwon Do with over two decades of experience in healing. She was born to build a revolution of brave healers who are getting their badass, authentic voices published in order to heal the world with their words. Find her programs, podcast, books and free Facebook group for healers at www.BraveHealer.com

A PASSION FOR THE HEALTH OF THE SEA

Aaron Kapner, Ceo, GreenKap Corp

As a busy New Yorker, GreenKap Corp founder and CEO Aaron Kapner has little time to devote to his favorite hobby. Wanting a more successful day on the water, he searched for a modern product to increase his fishing success. Aaron realized that in the history of fishing, the only major breakthrough inventions were a pole, a reel, a hook, and smelly, messy fish attractants. He set out to design a new effective attractant product that would be powerfully potent, clean and green, and fun. Concerned for our future, Aaron wanted his product to be entirely natural, providing only beneficial nutrients to the ecosystem, not unwanted chemicals. He wanted to take away the "yuck" factor of typical baits, chums, and oils, and add an element of fun, a product anyone could enjoy using. Using conventional fishing knowledge and a scientific breakthrough, Aaron created a dry-to-the-touch, lightweight, easily transported and stored, concentrated effervescing ball attractant.

But what is a state-of-the-art attractant without a matching delivery system?

Aaron then developed a revolutionary lure to dispense the chum right where you need it, at the hook! Aaron is solely responsible for the concepts of Chum Ballz and Chum Lures and has personally established key relationships that enabled him to bring his dream from design to market.He is now developing other potential sea-changing products, drawn from his passion for the health of the sea and our world. See the website: greenkaps.com.

Get Involved
ADOPT-A-PUFFIN!

Adopt one or more of Project Puffin's Atlantic Puffins, some of which our staff have studied for 35 years or more! With each $100 (tax-deductible) adoption, you will receive the following items:

- **Certificate of Adoption**: A colorful certificate displaying your name.
- **Biography**: Includes detailed information gathered by our researchers about an individual puffin from the time it hatched to the present; a summary of the puffin's most recent behavior, nesting, and other activities; and a current color picture.
- **Project Puffin book**: The option of receiving the book: Project Puffin: How We Brought Puffins Back to Egg Rock by Stephen Kress.

We will send you a renewal letter when it is time to renew your adoption.

GO TO:
http://projectpuffin.audubon.org/get-involved/adopt-puffin

The mission of Project Puffin is advancing the science of seabird conservation while encouraging protection and appreciation of seabirds worldwide.

TECHNIQUES TO TRY
...and tools to use

For the paper used in this book, watercolor is not recommended. Colored pencils or crayons will work well, and they don't smudge.

Chalk pastels provide beautiful colors, and you can buy a "smudge stick" to spread and blend the colors. But you also <u>must</u> have a can of spray fixative ready to secure, or 'fix" the chalk on the paper when you are finished working each session, so it doesn't smudge. Carefully follow the instructions on the can, and lightly spray outdoors, not indoors!

Try to buy sheet or package of 'glassine' paper, a thin, slick translucent paper that will protect your coloring pages while you work. It will prevent smudging when you close the book.

Another technique, my favorite, is to SEAL THE PAPER so you can use oil pastels, available at any art store. With these colors, you can use a brush and bit of painting medium to blend, thin out and spread the colors.

IE, you can put a line of dark blue at the top of the sky area and with some medium on a brush, pull , or lightly scrub the color down the page with a side to side motion. The pigment will thin out and get lighter as you pull it down, and it will give the sky a realistic, far away look. (You can do the same with the chalk pastels and the smudge stick).

To seal the paper, you will need: 7 metal "bulldog" clips, 2 ½" wide, a small bottle of acrylic matt medium, a 1 1/2" or 2" brush, a 1/2 " brush, a jar of water and some paper towels.

Clipping the drawing page and all the pages behind it, place 2 at the top and bottom of the page about 5" apart, and 3 along the side, to tightly secure the drawing page.

Dampen the brush, don't soak it, dip just the edge up to about 1/4" into the matt medium, and quickly brush it across the paper in 1 direction to within 1/2" of the edge of the page. Repeat over new areas until the page is covered. Do not brush over the same area twice.

Let this dry for 2-3 hours. The paper should not be wrinkled if this is done quickly , with the brush not being too wet. If it is a bit wrinkled, put a piece of writing paper or something thin and flat over the page close the book and put a weight on top if it. By the next day, it should be flat. Best if you cover the page with glassine first. Also make sure the page is dry before closing the book.

You can repeat with a 2nd coat after the page is dry. Now you have a sealed page that will work with oil pastels.

Make sure to rinse the acrylic medium off the brush with water as soon as you are done, or it will dry hard and ruin the brush.

You can purchase a small set of oil pastels along with the other supplies mentioned here in any art store, or on Amazon.

To paint with the oil pastels, first apply a color on a small area, perhaps the sky area as it is a large open space, and with a smaller , flat brush about 1/2" wide, try blending the color moving the brush side to side and downward. You can work out a technique after just a few minutes of trying this. It is really fun and will inspire you to do more.

You can use the side of the brush to color small or thin areas, or have some colored pencils right there for very small areas. You might want to have a very thin brush as well for the small areas.

If you've never done this before, please take a deep breath, maybe twice, shake off any apprehensions, and feel free.

The Kabuki drawing here, even in gray scale, shows you the range of possibilities using oil pastels as well as chalk pastels. Some areas are blended, some are just hit with the side of the pastel and not blended. And you can see that you can leave some areas open as just line. Feel free to be creative.

Most of the artwork on my website is done with this oil pastel technique, so please take a look at these to pick up some ideas about how you can color the birds.

Toward the end of August we will have a technique video on the website. Let us know if you are interested, and we will notify you when the video is posted, and also send you a digital image of another beautiful bird drawing you can download and color and frame. Email the studio: Seabird@hamptonsartist.com

Lynn Matsuoka
www.hamptonsartist.com

ABOUT THE ARTIST

Lynn Matsuoka is internationally known for her drawings & paintings of Japan's ancient arts of Sumo and Kabuki, as performed today. She has also garnered the Hawaii Publisher's Association First Prize for Illustration for her powerful paintings of Hawaii's hula dancers.

Matsuoka, a New York native, studied music and art at Temple University in Philadelphia and graduated with a BFA Degree. She went on to study graduate drawing at the School of Visual Arts in Manhattan with famed artist Jack Potter.

Her work so captures the essence of the subject matter that print and broadcast media have used her art reportage skills repeatedly to enhance their publications and broadcasts. As a court reportage artist for ABC and CBS network news, she covered many court trials, most notably as a court illustrator for the Watergate hearings.

In Manhattan, Matsuoka started her career as a fashion illustrator for major department stores and covered fashion shows in New York and Tokyo for *Vogue* magazine and *Women's Wear Daily*. Her illustrations have also appeared in the *Wall Street Journal*, *Time*, *Business Week* as well as other publications.

When invited to Tokyo to be a fashion illustrator for a major Japanese department store, she discovered Sumo and devoted a large part of her focus to the sport. She's spent decades documenting the tournaments, the practice ring, and the rural and international tours. Matsuoka has also intensively covered the world of Kabuki. From behind the scenes she captures the spirit of the actors in intimate detail. The artist has covered Yankees Spring trainings and works with Equestrian events.

Matsuoka lives and works in the Hamptons, NY, where she has turned her considerable talent to raising funds for endangered species through efforts like this book. You can view her webpage at https://hamptonsartist.com or contact her directly at artist@hamptonsartist.com

YOUR NOTES AND SKETCHES

Made in the USA
Middletown, DE
01 July 2019